EAT LIKE
A LOCAL-
NEW YORK

New York State Food Guide

Denise Lacey-Corcoran

Cover designed by: Lisa Rusczyk Ed. D.

CZYK Publishing Since 2011.

Eat Like a Local

Lock Haven, PA
All rights reserved.
ISBN: 9798697282984

BOOK DESCRIPTION

Are you excited about planning your next trip? Do you want an edible experience? Would you like some culinary guidance from a local? If you answered yes to any of these questions, then this Eat Like a Local book is for you. Eat Like a Local - New York State by Denise Lacey-Corcoran offers the inside scoop on food in New York State. Culinary tourism is an important aspect of any travel experience. Food has the ability to tell you a story of a destination, its landscapes, and culture on a single plate. Most food guides tell you how to eat like a tourist. Although there is nothing wrong with that, as part of the Eat Like a Local series, this book will give you a food guide from someone who has lived at your next culinary destination.

In these pages, you will discover advice on having a unique edible experience. This book will not tell you exact addresses or hours but instead will give you excitement and knowledge of food and drinks from a local that you may not find in other travel food guides.

Eat like a local. Slow down, stay in one place, and get to know the food, people, and culture. By the time you finish this book, you will be eager and prepared to travel to your next culinary destination.

OUR STORY

Traveling has always been a passion of the creator of the Eat Like a Local book series. During Lisa's travels in Malta, instead of tasting what the city offered, she ate at a large fast-food chain. However, she realized that her traveling experience would have been more fulfilling if she had experienced the best of local cuisines. Most would agree that food is one of the most important aspects of a culture. Through her travels, Lisa learned how much locals had to share with tourists, especially about food. Lisa created the Eat Like a Local book series to help connect people with locals which she discovered is a topic that locals are very passionate about sharing. So please join me and: Eat, drink, and explore like a local.

TABLE OF CONTENTS

DEDICATION

This book is dedicated to LPC. Thanks for being you.

ABOUT THE AUTHOR

Denise Lacey-Corcoran is a music educator, who lives with her family in Upstate New York. She is also an avid genealogist, who often convinces her family to take a stroll through an old cemetery because you never know who you might find! Many of her trips also include locations for learning about family history and learning about how her ancestors might have lived. The joy of finding the missing link that solves a family mystery is thrilling! One of her fondest travel memories is sitting outside on a bench, in the tiny village that her family came from in Ireland, talking with an elderly village historian.

Denise loves exploring off the beaten path locations when she is traveling, seeking out places that tourists do not typically go to. Her favorite places to explore are the Irish countryside, the Outer Cape of Cape Cod, Prince Edward Island, England, and NYC. When she and her family are not traversing distant locations, they like to explore their own region of the Finger Lakes. Even after living in the region her entire life, Denise still finds new nature preserves to hike, new places to kayak, and of course, new foodie destinations!

HOW TO USE THIS BOOK

The goal of this book is to help culinary travelers either dream or experience different edible experiences by providing opinions from a local. The author has made suggestions based on their own knowledge. Please do your own research before traveling to the area in case the suggested locations are unavailable.

Travel Advisories: As a first step in planning any trip abroad, check the Travel Advisories for your intended destination.
https://travel.state.gov/content/travel/en/traveladvisories/traveladvisories.html

FROM THE PUBLISHER

Traveling can be one of the most important parts of a person's life. The anticipation and memories that you have are some of the best. As a publisher of the *Eat Like a Local*, Greater Than a Tourist, as well as the popular *50 Things to Know* book series, we strive to help you learn about new places, spark your imagination, and inspire you. Wherever you are and whatever you do I wish you safe, fun, and inspiring travel.

Lisa Rusczyk Ed. D.
CZYK Publishing

"People who love to eat are always the best people."

- Julia Child

I truly believe this quote from the whit of Julia Child! At first, you might laugh, and think how silly it is because all people eat. But do they really *enjoy* eating and appreciate food? Do they allow themselves to truly experience a location through the food, or do they flock to the nearest chain restaurant?

For me, traveling is all about learning as much as I can about a location, talking to people, and appreciating local experiences. Engaging with local people is the way to find the freshest fish markets, farmers markets, and the best whole in the wall restaurants. Please try to embrace the idea that reaching out and talking with people is one of your best resources, and that those conversations can become some of your treasured travel memories. I'm not saying that you should always go blindly into a trip without researching anything and solely rely on asking local people their opinions. Admittedly, I research extensively before most trips, read reviews, and come up with a basic plan. However, I find if I over plan, and have a rigid itinerary, I miss out on the spontaneity which is part of what makes traveling so fun.

So why should you visit NYS? Some people hear "New York" and immediately think of New York City. Countless times when we have been traveling, someone asks us where we're from, we say "New York," and they assume New York City. New York City is one of my favorite places to visit, but it is definitely not representative of all of New York State. The varying regions of New York State have something for all travelers, from lakes, mountains, and small towns, to bustling cities.

You may be thinking about spending a week, a weekend, or a day in New York. I encourage you to use the suggestions in this book as a jumping-off point. Perhaps you choose an eatery that sounds good to you, then plan on exploring the town a little further. Supporting small, family-owned businesses is crucial to a small village's economy and the local tourism industry. After you've had that amazing lunch, grab a latte from the local coffeehouse and take time to meander through the surrounding boutiques, art galleries, and bookstores. But most importantly when you're traveling, slow down, relax, and take time to truly enjoy life!

New York
USA

New York Climate

	High	Low
January	39	26
February	43	29
March	52	36
April	64	45
May	72	54
June	80	64
July	84	69
August	84	69
September	76	61
October	64	50
November	55	42
December	44	31

GreaterThanaTourist.com

Temperatures are in Fahrenheit degrees.
Source: NOAA

1. NEW YORK STATE (NYS) WEATHER

The old joke about NYS weather is that you could experience all four seasons in one day! Well, maybe not one day, but definitely in one week! Parts of New York may see snow anywhere from October to May. New York City will always be the warmest place in NYS, with the temperature typically decreasing as you travel further Upstate. I would highly encourage you to pack an umbrella, light rain jacket, and sweater/sweatshirt even if you are traveling during the summer months. This is a great chance to pack your flannel shirt for an evening around the campfire in the Adirondacks or Catskills!

2. GETTING AROUND NYS

Public transportation in the larger cities is great, reliable, and inexpensive but not in the more rural parts of the state. If you are staying in NYC, definitely plan on leaving your car at home, or parking it for the duration of your trip. However, if you are exploring the rich outdoor activities that Upstate New York has to offer, be sure that you have a car. Once you get to a smaller location, you can

13

typically park your car and enjoy walking around the
village, without the hassle of driving everywhere.
Some cities (large and small) offer bike and kayak
rentals as additional options for touring.

3. DRESS CODE

The majority of the restaurants mentioned in this
book are casual. You can certainly dress more
formally if you would like, but it generally isn't
necessary. I have noted within each section which
restaurants you might like to dress business casual,
instead of jeans and Birkenstocks! If you're
concerned about the dress code, just call ahead and
ask. I find that it is better to call than show up and
feel uncomfortable during the entire meal!

4. CURRENCY AND TIPPING

The majority of restaurants in NYS will take credit
cards. Some smaller businesses will not accept
American Express, so be sure to have another credit
card handy. Many businesses at farmers markets now
accept credit cards, as well. However, when
shopping at a farmers market, I always carry cash just

in case. You will want to have smaller bills with you if you plan on purchasing items from roadside stands.

Tipping is expected at all but fast-food restaurants in NYS. Many restaurants now have the tip figured out for you in increments of 15%, 18%, and 20%, when you are presented with a credit card payment screen or a bill. Generally, it is customary to tip more toward 18% or 20%. If the tip is not figured out for you, a good trick is to double the tax and add a little bit more.

5. TASTE NY STORES

Taste NY Stores are a great opportunity to sample many products produced in New York State. They are located in a variety of locations across New York, from Grand Central Station to the North Country. Each regional Taste NY Store will sell different products that are produced in that specific area. We find it is fun to explore a store, get some snacks for the drive, or even the ingredients for an entire meal.

6. GROCERY STORES

In my opinion, the best grocery store chain in NYS is Wegmans. Along with typical grocery items, their stores offer exceptionally fresh produce, many organic items, and a cafe. Wegmans stores range in size, but larger ones offer indoor and outdoor seating areas where you can enjoy your sushi, vegetarian specialties, and more. In larger cities, Trader Joe's and Whole Foods are trusted favorites. Co-ops such as Greenstar Natural Food Market, in Ithaca, will offer locally grown and prepared foods. Whatever town you visit, try to search out small, family-owned markets that will give you a taste of the community. A note about alcohol sales in NYS - Grocery stores sell beer, hard cider, and hard seltzer. If you would like wine or spirits, you will need to go to the local liquor store.

7. FIRST FRIDAY

First Fridays are a fun way to explore new towns! Many NYS towns and villages hold First Fridays on the first Friday of every month, from April-December. Towns often have a central location, usually the tourism office or Chamber of Commerce, where you can pick up a listing of the evening's events. First Fridays typically include free musical performances, menu specials at restaurants, later shopping hours, gallery openings, historical society events, and children's activities. First Fridays are a relaxing way to spend a Friday evening experiencing new things and meeting local people!

8. NEW YORK STATE'S SPECIALTY FOODS

There are several foods that originated in New York State. In this section, you will find a description of each mouthwatering treat, and where to find them in your travels.

Spiedies - Spiedies are basically heavily marinated shish kabobs made from chicken (my favorite), beef, lamb, or pork. They originated in the Southern Tier of NY, where people have traditionally enjoyed spiedie sandwiches, salads, and subs. The best place to sample spiedies is at Lupo's Spiedies in Endicott or Binghamton. If you love their sauce you can purchase it at their restaurants or local grocery stores. There is a recipe for our family Spiedie Marinade in the Bonus tips.

Dinosaur Bar-B-Que - This restaurant's claim to fame is their slow-roasted meats and amazing Bar-B-Que sauce. The original restaurant is in Syracuse, but there are now six other locations all over NYS. Dinosaur Bar-B-Que sauce can be purchased at their restaurants and at many grocery stores.

Bazoobie - The Bazoobie is an enormous, warm, chocolate chip cookie. Residents in the North Country and students at SUNY Potsdam and Clarkson

University have loved Bazoobies for decades. If you want to try one of your own, swing by The Bagelry, in Potsdam.

<u>Garbage Plate</u> - The Garbage Plate originated in Rochester, and has a few variations from traditional to vegetarian/vegan. The most traditional Garbage Plate will contain french fries topped with baked beans, chili, hotdogs, onions, and mustard. This is a huge plate of food, and gained popularity with late-night eating college students.

<u>Buffalo Wings</u> - No surprise here, buffalo wings originated in Buffalo. Buffalo wings are deep-fried chicken wings coated in a spicy sauce and are often served with blue cheese dressing. Every location that serves buffalo wings has its own special recipe for the spicy sauce.

<u>Thousand Island Dressing</u> - The story of how Thousand Island dressing was created has been clouded over time, and a few variations exist. Some attribute the recipe to Sophia Lelonde, who was the wife of a fishing guide in the late 1800s. Other stories attribute the recipe to Oschar Tschirky, the chef of George Boldt, who was the owner of New York City's Waldorf Astoria hotel. Regardless of who created Thousand Island dressing, it soon became popular all over the country. The dressing contains ketchup, mayonnaise, sweet relish, onions, garlic, white vinegar, and salt. River Rat Cheese, in Clayton, sells authentic Thousand Island Dressing, made from the original recipe.

9. MAPLE MOLASSES, PANCAKE SYRUP, OR LIQUID GOLD

No matter what you call it, maple syrup has legendarily been a NYS tradition dating back to early Iroquois times. Today, there are over 2,000 producers of maple syrup in New York. The Sugar Maple is even New York's state tree. Pure maple syrup can take on a different taste depending upon where it is harvested and the type of Maple tree that is tapped. In general, the darker the syrup, the stronger the flavors. The grades are Light Amber, Medium, Dark, and Extra Dark, with the color darkening and maple flavor intensifying at each level. When you are driving around rural parts of NYS, look for lines (they often look like multi-colored hoses) stretching from wooded areas to collection tanks near homes or sugaring huts. You can purchase locally produced maple syrup at most farm stores, Taste NY stores, and some grocery stores. My favorite maple syrup

producer tucked away on a dirt road is Hamley's Maple Farm, in Barton. This family-owned farm offers pancake breakfasts and tours in the early Spring. On your way to Hamley's, be sure to look for the old one-room schoolhouse just down the road! There is a website dedicated to NYS Maple that offers information on other farms to visit and several maple recipes.

10. FOOD TRANSLATIONS FOR NEW YORK STATE

Yes, different regions of NYS have different names for certain foods. Here are the three that seem to cause the most befuddlement!

Pop vs Soda - In Rochester, Buffalo, and the Western part of the state, people call carbonated, sugary beverages, "pop." The rest of the state calls it "soda."

Sub vs Hero - In Upstate NY, a sandwich on a long roll, filled with meats, cheeses, veggies, and condiments is called a sub. New York City, Long Island, and a few of the downstate counties refer to the sandwich as a hero.

<u>Schmear vs just asking for cream cheese</u> - A schmear is a thick spread of cream cheese (sometimes flavored) on a New York City bagel. When you're in Upstate NY, just ask for cream cheese, but when you're in NYC, ask for a schmear. Insider tip - The chewy goodness of a boiled NYC bagel should be enjoyed as is, not toasted.

11. FARM STORES

New York State has an abundance of farm stores, not to be confused with farmers markets. They are two very different and separate entities. Farmers markets have booths with many different farmers and craftspeople, while farm stores are a single store located on or near a farm. I love to go to various farm stores and source as many local products as possible. Be advised that farm stores often have different hours than a typical store. Their hours may also change depending on the season. I would highly encourage you to check their Facebook pages or websites for more information.

A few of my favorite farm stores:

Fly Creek Cider Mill and Orchards, in Fly Creek, offers an abundance of free samples of their foods. In addition to cider, hard cider, and various apple products, they also sell their own marinades, pickled vegetables, and mustards.

Engelberts Farm Store and Creamery, in Nichols, is a wonderful family-owned farm and store stocked full of all organic products. Engelberts produce their own organic beef, pork, cheeses, and produce. They also sell many other local organic products.

Side Hill Acres, in Candor, is a tiny farm store, tucked into the countryside. They specialize in many different flavors of goat cheese. Side Hill Acres also sells goat meat and goat milk soaps and lotions. Sometimes they even let customers visit their goats!

12. FARMERS MARKETS

Farmers Markets are one of my favorite places to go during any season. My favorite market is Ithaca Farmers Market, overlooking Cayuga Lake Inlet. The open-air market, which is only open on weekends, is filled with local artisans, farmers, chefs, vintners, and brewers. You can easily spend the day shopping, eating lunch by the lake, and listening to eclectic music. Delicious lunch options at the market include Macro Mama's for vegetarian and seasonal foods (be sure to try their peanut lime noodles), Veronika's Pastries for sweet and savory crepes, and Just Desserts for wood-fired pizzas. Ithaca Farmers Market often hosts unique events like the Rutabaga Curl!

The Broome County Regional Farmers Market is housed in a wonderful new building in Binghamton. This market is open year-round, with farm offerings changing depending on the season. Great foodie offerings here include Java Joe's Roasting Company, Despina's Mediterranean Taste, Old Barn Market, and Bread in the Wild (see the bakery section for more information).

CNY Regional Market in Syracuse is held inside several large buildings and is open year-round. They offer local favorites such as cheese, fried dough, and grape products, as well as wholesale produce from across the country. You can grab lunch at the market or go across the street to the many restaurants at Destiny USA.

13. WINERIES

People may think of California as the wine capital of the US, but the vineyards of New York are also superb. There are numerous wineries in New York State, but some of the best are located in the Finger Lakes region. Each vineyard has its own unique twist to tastings, food offerings, and music. Most wineries will ask you to pay a small fee for tastings. I would encourage you to check the vineyards' websites for special events.

Insider tip - Wineries are a popular destination in the Summer and Fall, but most are also open in the Winter. During January-March, wineries are far less crowded, so you often can enjoy a more one-on-one experience with the vintner.

Some of my favorite vineyards are:

Bully Hill Vineyards, in Hammondsport, is well-known for its fun tastings! Their tasting fee includes a souvenir wine glass and a small plate of food. Bully Hill wines feature creative labels, with fun names, including Love My Goat and Sweet Walter.

Lucas Vineyards in Interlaken has a fabulous Gewurztraminer, along with other local favorites such as TugBoat Red and their Nautie series. If you are in the Finger Lakes region in early September, try to spend an afternoon at Lucas Vineyards German Festival. This is a family-friendly event with a Bavarian Band, grape stomping, and all sorts of German food.

Thirsty Owl Wine Company, in Ovid, is one of the few wineries that has access to Cayuga Lake and allows visitors to dock their boats. They have a wonderful bistro with great salads and sandwiches.

Glenora Wine Cellars, in Dundee, runs a lovely inn and restaurant at their vineyard. Glenora offers many special events including their Leaves and Lobster Festival in September and their champagne making class on New Year's Eve.

14. BREWERIES

There are an abundance of breweries in NYS and even a Beer Trail. You could easily plan a trip to many regions of NYS solely based on visiting different breweries.

Favorite breweries around NYS include:

Ithaca Beer Co. is a family-owned brewery located in Ithaca, in the heart of the Finger Lakes. Local favorites include Flower Power, Apricot Wheat, and Nut Brown Ale. When visiting Ithaca Beer, younger members of your group can enjoy Ginger Beer or Root Beer, brewed on the premises. They also offer wood-fired pizzas and sandwiches at their cafe.

Saranac Brewery in Utica was founded in 1888. They are known for their fun brewery tours, ending with a glass of their beer. Children may enjoy one of their seven types of soda, including Shirley Temple or Black Cherry Cream sodas. Adults enjoy perennial favorites such as Adirondack Lager and Octoberfest.

The Brewery Ommegang in Cooperstown offers Belgian-style beers. Brewery Ommegang is housed in a beautiful facility that includes a cafe, tasting room, and visitors center. They offer tours and tastings daily and host a large beer festival in July.

Favorites at Ommegang include Hennepin, Three Philosophers, and the Game of Thrones-themed beers.

Binghamton Brewing Company in Johnson City is one of the newer craft breweries in New York State. Interestingly, the owners have repurposed an old Endicott Johnson & Co. Fire Company building, into the brewery. If you're unfamiliar with the Endicott Johnson Company and plan to visit the Southern Tier, I would encourage you to look up their history! Their beers are made from locally sourced malt and hops and can be tasted in their taproom. They produce about ten types of beer ranging from an Amber Ale to a Coffee Dry stout.

All of the breweries mentioned here, except Binghamton Brewing Company, sell their beers and sodas in many grocery stores. Please see the pub section for information on Ellicottville Brewery, in the Chautauqua- Allegheny region.

15. DINERS

NYS boasts many vintage diners that will take you back in time with their decor and friendly staff. In my opinion, great diners need to have top-notch all-day breakfast items, and offer a clean dining and bathroom experience! Here are a few that fit the bill: Crazy Otto's Empire Diner, in Herkimer, serves enormous and delicious omelets, as well as other breakfast and lunch favorites. Many locals go there every day for their favorite dishes. The decor includes vintage photos of *I Love Lucy* and *Howdy Doody*. Broadway Diner, in Endwell, as the name suggests, is decorated with NYC themed decor and a variety of Broadway musical posters. They are open for breakfast, lunch, and dinner. Expect to wait on the weekends, as the breakfast crowd is huge! Traveling downstate, Roscoe Diner is a fixture on old Route 17C, in Roscoe. They serve everything from breakfast staples to Bison Burgers. This is definitely a favorite stop when one is driving from Upstate to NYC!

16. PUBS

A great pub combines a comfortable, friendly atmosphere, with good food and drink. Coleman's Irish Pub, on Syracuse's Tipperary Hill, is a unique establishment, with both human and leprechaun size front doors and phone booths! When you walk in Coleman's, you feel as though you have been transported to a different time period and a different country. They have typical Irish pub favorites such as Bangers and Mash and Guinness Stew, along with local favorites like Gianelli sausage. If you go to Coleman's, be sure to look for the upside-down traffic light (with the green on top), at the corner of Milton Avenue and Tompkins Street! Traveling to the Western part of NYS, Market Street Brewing Co. in Corning has been brewing beer and serving great food for over 20 years. Here you could drink their D'Artagnan Dark Ale while enjoying a Southwest Salad or a Quinoa Black Bean Burger. Proceeding further West, Ellicottville Brewing Company, with pubs in Ellicottville, Fredonia, Bemus Point is a great place to eat if you are traveling near Jamestown or checking out SUNY Fredonia. Their pubs have a relaxed feeling where you can order a pint of

Blueberry Maple Pancake Beer while enjoying a goat cheese salad, fish tacos, or a burger.

17. GOOD FOR FAMILIES

We have always taken our daughter everywhere, and I believe every restaurant mentioned in this book is child friendly. However, if you have a larger family, there are a few tried and true favorites. Mario's Pizza, in Owego, has been family owned and operated for decades, serving amazing Italian food. You really cannot go wrong with anything on the menu. Their pizza, subs, and pasta are all fantastic, and the servings are plentiful. Children and those with smaller appetites might want to order a half order of their pasta! Traveling toward the Capital Region, Brooks House of Barbecue in Oneonta has been family owned since 1951. Our family considers it the best barbecue chicken in NYS. Their sauces can be purchased at the restaurant or at many NYS grocery stores. If you arrive at Brooks during peak summer hours (especially when there are events going on at the Baseball Hall of Fame in Cooperstown) be ready for a wait. Insider tip - The wait for sitting at the counter is generally much shorter than waiting for a table or booth. Just send one of your party to the check-in podium and ask if counter space is available. In the Finger Lakes Region, Viva Taqueria, in Ithaca, is a brightly decorated, fast-paced Mexican restaurant. They have indoor and outdoor seating, where nobody cares how loud you are! The meals are all freshly prepared, with vegan and vegetarian options. Viva Taqueria's extensive menu of Mexican favorites is sure to have something that will satisfy everyone in your group!

18. GREAT DATE NIGHT

Sometimes a great date night can mean staying home, ordering pizza, and watching a movie, but sometimes you want something a little more. Just a Taste, in Ithaca, is one of our favorite places for a special night out. This cozy restaurant, with an outside patio, serves tapas (small plates to share) made from seasonal ingredients. The menu changes frequently. They also have an extensive wine list, with several wine flights. Be sure to arrive early, as the line for dinner often starts a half hour before they open. If you have to wait, it will be worth it! Also in the Finger Lakes Region, is Dano's Heuringer on

Seneca, in Lodi. Dano's is modeled after a traditional Viennese Winery Restaurant. Their rotating menu features Viennese spreads and artisanal breads, salads, vegetable dishes, homemade sausages, seafood, and Viennese pastries. They also have an extensive wine list. At a Heuringer, menu items are ordered a la carte, either all at once or as the meal progresses. Dano's definitely offers a unique and special dining experience to all of their customers. If you are in NYC, Rosemary's, in the West Village is a lovely spot for a glass of wine and a delicious meal. They serve fresh Italian specialties prepared from produce harvested from their rooftop garden and Upstate farm. You could dress casually at all of the restaurants in this section, but you could also wear business casual and be very comfortable.

19. BRUNCH

Weekend brunch always seems like a lovely indulgent treat to me! DeWitt Cafe, in Ithaca, is located in DeWitt Mall, which is a repurposed building that once housed Ithaca High School. They offer a very relaxed and warm setting, enabling guests to take their time and enjoy the delicious food. Some of my favorites include the Tunisian plate (with their amazing apple carrot chutney) and the Brioche french toast. DeWitt Cafe does not take credit cards, so be sure to have cash with you. In Central New York, The Cellar Restaurant located on River Row in Owego has long been a fixture in the brunch world. They have an indoor dining room, as well as a deck that overlooks the Susquehanna River. Their brunch specialties include five different types of Eggs Benedict, Filet Mignon and Lobster Hash, as well as various sandwiches and seasonal salads. Traveling to the Capital Region, Sweet Mimi's Cafe and Bakery, in Saratoga Springs, is located in the historic Caffe Lena Building. Brunch items range from an assortment of pancakes and scones to creative omelets and breakfast sandwiches. You can also pick up dessert, or breakfast goods for the next morning, on your way out!

20. VEGETARIAN/VEGAN

We love eating vegetarian and try to eat as many meatless meals as possible. Many restaurants offer vegetarian and/or vegan options, but it's fun to explore restaurants that are completely vegetarian/vegan, as well. One of our favorite vegetarian restaurants is Moosewood in DeWitt Mall, in Ithaca. Moosewood is a collectively owned business that has been a fixture in vegetarian cooking for over 45 years. Their menu changes frequently, featuring favorites such as Indian Curry, Caribbean Vegetable Stew, and Thai Butternut Squash Soup. They have an extensive list of both alcoholic and non-alcoholic beverages. Ginger tea and Superfantastics are a couple of our favorites! In the Southern Tier, Parlor City Vegan, in Binghamton, is a newer business that started out with a booth at the Broome County Farmers Market. They are now housed in a beautiful, old building in Binghamton's Antique Row. The husband and wife team make all of their nut cheeses in house. Their specialties range from the Skeptical Vegan (truffle mac and cheese, topped with housemade ranch dressing, BBQ sauce, and bacon bits) to Ruthie's Buttermilk Chicken Biscuit (housemade fried chicken seitan, buttermilk biscuit, hot sauce, and pickles). Their Lox on a bagel, with lox made from carrots and nut cream cheese tastes just like its non-vegan counterpart! Traveling down to NYC, Blossom, in Greenwich Village, is a more up-scale vegan establishment. Their trendy location offers a variety of exquisitely prepared meals, ranging from sandwiches to pizza to main dishes.

21. FARM TO TABLE

Farm to Table restaurants have gained in popularity over the last few years, with more people craving fresh, local foods. Most Farm to Table restaurants quickly gain a local following and serve any number of creative, seasonal dishes. The first two restaurants in this category, can both be found in the Finger Lakes region. The first is Hazelnut Kitchen, in Trumansburg. This eatery uses only locally sourced farm ingredients, so their menu changes based on the availability of foods. They serve many vegetarian dishes and unique desserts. Agava, in Ithaca, is a farm to table restaurant that serves Southwest-inspired cuisine. The restaurant prides itself on being a community-minded and friendly place to dine. They are known for their wood-fired flatbreads and have vegan and gluten-free options. Agava also serves beer and spirits from local breweries and distilleries. If you are traveling in the Hudson Valley region, American Bounty Restaurant, in Hyde Park, is a popular choice at The Culinary Institute of America. Student chefs, overseen by faculty chefs, focus on seasonal and regional products, in order to celebrate American cuisine. They partner with many local farms to provide customers with the freshest food possible. There are several high-quality restaurants at The Culinary Institute of America.

22. U-PICK FARM FUN

There are numerous small and large u-pick farms all across NYS, where you can pick a wide range of produce. Most larger u-pick farms will take credit cards, and will offer you containers/bags to use for picking. Some farms will encourage you to have your own reusable bags in an effort to reduce waste. If you, like me, are concerned with what is sprayed on my food, call the farms ahead of time and ask about their pest management system. Some may use integrated pest management and some may be completely organic.

There are some simple, but important rules to remember when you are visiting a u-pick farm. First of all, remember that the products you are picking are what a family relies on for their livelihood. Please only pick what you are going to keep. Try to avoid picking something, taking one bite, and throwing it down. If you do sample something, eat the entire item. If you do not care for it, please have a small bag with you to carry out your garbage, instead of throwing it on the ground. Another common courtesy to remember is that if you come upon another group picking in a certain spot, please try not to crowd them. Chances are you can go to another tree/bush farther down the row and find items that are just as good. There's nothing more annoying than when you are happily picking apples with your family, and another group starts picking from the same tree! Basically, you need to follow the rules of the farm, and please only pick what they tell you is currently ready to be harvested. The peach in the next row over might look amazing, but if the farm tells you that row isn't quite ripe yet, please believe them.

Indian Creek in Ithaca, dubbed "Ithaca's Orchard Playground," is one of our favorite u-pick farms.

This is a relaxed, quirky farm, with a helpful and knowledgeable staff. You could spend the entire day roaming the orchards and flower and vegetable gardens. They offer a variety of u-pick flowers, vegetables, and fruits, depending on the time of year. I encourage you to check out their fun website and blog for more information. Also in the Finger Lakes Region, Littletree Orchards, in Newfield, is a small family-owned farm, operating since the early 1970s. This farm is near to my heart, as I have many fond childhood memories of crisp fall days filled with apple picking and eating picnic lunches at Littletree. As the name implies, all of their trees are quite small, making it easier for little ones to reach the apples. Littletree is known for their u-pick apples, but sometimes they offer other u-pick fruits, as well. Their quaint farm store, housed in an old barn, is stocked with housemade cider, applesauce, herbal apple cider vinegar (a great gift to take to someone back home), and warm cider donuts.

Traveling into the Southern Tier, Gary's Berries, in Campville, is a small family-owned blueberry farm. Gary's entire family pitches in and works during the July blueberry season. They offer repurposed coffee cans, lined with plastic bags, and rope handles, for you to use for picking. This is a fun family activity that will allow you to pick several pounds of blueberries in an hour! When you check out, be sure to notice their "Sin Bin." This is a box you can throw your change in to pay for the blueberries that you ate while you were picking. At the end of the season, all of the "Sin Bin" money goes to a local charity. Note that this farm only takes cash or checks. Another u-pick farm a little further East is Apple Hills Farm. Located in the hills of Binghamton, their orchards offer beautiful views of the surrounding area. They specialize in u-pick blueberries (July) and apples (September). Their Apple Dumpling Cafe serves fantastic breakfast and lunch options, along with homemade breads, doughnuts, and cookies. Traveling North, further into Central NY, Beak and Skiff Apple Orchards, in LaFayette, is a large farm that offers u-pick apples. Sometimes you can even catch a wagon ride out to the orchards! On the property, you can also visit their general store, bakery, and distillery. Their 1911 Tasting Room and Tavern serves their own hard cider, vodka, and gin.

A relatively newfound u-pick option for my family is grapes! There are many farms in the Finger Lakes Region, especially around Seneca, Keuka, and Canandaigua Lakes. Wandering through a vineyard, with lake views, on a sunny Fall day, is a relaxing way to spend an afternoon! I would suggest taking your own scissors to cut the bunches of grapes. Some vineyards will provide picking containers and clippers, but to be on the safe side, we always take our own. The grape season is fairly short, so always call ahead or check out vineyard websites and social media posts for updates on picking. Some of the farms offer seedless grapes but most only grow seeded. Lilly Family Farm, in Hector, offers many seedless varieties. Glendale Farm, in Burdett, offers many varieties of organic grapes, with breathtaking views of Seneca Lake.

23. COFFEE HOUSES ARE MY FAVORITE!

I love discovering a funky coffeehouse during my travels! Wandering in a new cozy little place, smelling the enticing coffee, and hearing acoustic music is always a treat when I'm on vacation! One of my favorite coffeehouses is Strange Brew, in Binghamton, which has an artsy college town vibe. The friendly baristas make it a point to learn your name and usual order. They serve locally roasted Java

Joe's Roasting Company coffee, with seasonal flavors including, Dutch Apple Crumb and Blueberry Cinnamon Crumble. In addition to a wide range of coffee drinks, they also serve many flavors of bubble tea and smoothies. Strange Brew is also a fun spot for breakfast (which they serve all day) and lunch. Our favorite menu items include housemade soups, omelets, and macaroni and cheese. Just about 30 minutes down the road, you will find Carol's Coffee and Art Bar, in Owego. This coffeehouse has a small village vibe, which helps you feel instantly welcomed. Along with coffee drinks and yummy smoothies, Carol's also serves freshly made salads and sandwiches. There are also numerous gluten-free items. If you're in the mood for a treat, try the Coconut Cake! You will enjoy looking at all of Carol's paintings, while drinking your beverage, as well!

Traveling downstate, you might like to try Bank Square Coffee House in Beacon. I discovered this cute coffeehouse when I took the train back from Manhattan and wanted a drink for the drive home. Bank Square roasts their own delicious coffee right in Beacon. They also serve healthy smoothies and tempting baked goods.

In the Western part of NYS, is Crown Street Roasting Company, in Jamestown. The baristas there are very kind and they serve amazing lattes. Crown Street is a great place to go on your way to the Lucy-Desi Museum, which is right around the corner.

24. SO MAYBE TEA SHOPS ARE REALLY MY FAVORITE!

I am admittedly a tea snob. There's nothing better than a strong cup of tea, poured from a china teapot, into a beautiful teacup. I'm a firm believer that a good cup of tea can fix almost anything! When one refers to a tea shop, there are shops actually serving tea, and those that only sell tea to brew at home. This section will explore both options. In my opinion, the best British restaurant on the East Coast is Tea and Sympathy, in the West Village. This is my favorite place to eat, and get a cup of tea, in Manhattan. They serve a variety of loose teas, served in eclectic teapots, with china teacups. In addition to endless cups of tea and scrumptious afternoon teas, they also serve classic British breakfast, lunch, and dinner selections. I would highly recommend making reservations and reading Nikki's rules on the door before you go in! After enjoying tea, be sure to visit the shop next door for goodies to take home.

McNulty's Tea Shop is also in the West Village and has been selling teas since 1895. When you step in the small shop you are immediately engulfed in the intoxicating aromas of tea and coffee. The loose teas in apothecary jars and antique gold scales remind one of a by-gone era. McNulty's does not serve cups of tea or coffee but sells many teas and coffees to brew at home. Insider tip - This shop has been frequented by celebrities for years and some even have their own special tea blends. The blends are not advertised but are written on index cards, and housed behind the counter. If you ask the owners, they might just let you purchase your favorite actor's blend! For instance, Katherine Hepburn's blend makes a lovely cup of tea!

Alice's Teacup has three locations in NYC. They have an extensive list of teas, all served in beautiful china teapots. Alice's serves delightful breakfast, brunch, lunch, and afternoon tea selections. They have sweet and savory daily scone specials, as well. Reservations, especially on the weekends, are a good idea. Insider Tip - When you go to Alice's, you can request a pair of fairy wings for your little ones (or adults!) to wear during your meal. The wings are also accompanied by a sprinkling of fairy dust at your table!

25. CAFES

Along with coffeehouses, I always think it's fun to stumble upon a new little cafe, offering fresh and healthy foods! Not only do I enjoy exploring the menu items at cafes, but also the unique decorations and histories of the buildings. The Owego Kitchen, located in historic downtown Owego, is our go-to for lunch every Sunday (and some days in between, too). Soon after they opened, I told the owner The Owego Kitchen was the kind of place you find on vacation and wish you had one back home! They serve amazing breakfast sandwiches, fresh salads, and inventive sandwiches, along with a variety of baked goods and housemade soups. The Owego Kitchen also brews many flavors of hot and iced Finger Lakes Coffee Roasters coffee. You can check their Facebook page for daily soup, salad, and sandwich specials. Insider tip - If you decide to stay in Owego (which is a Historical National Register District and was named the Coolest Small Town in America), the owners of The Owego Kitchen also own The Belva

Lockwood Inn. The Inn is a bed and breakfast, housed in a beautifully renovated Victorian home. It is located on the property where Belva Lockwood once worked as a school principal. Belva was the first woman to argue before the Supreme Court and run for president.

While the Ithaca Bakery has "bakery" in its name, it is also a large, bustling cafe. They have an extensive menu featuring breakfast, lunch, and dinner with many vegetarian/vegan options. Along with unique sandwiches, they also have a seasonal menu with food and specialty drinks. This is a go-to stop for locals, college students, and visitors. You can eat in, or get your items to go and eat at one of Ithaca's many beautiful parks.

Elf in the Oak, in Burdett, is a great spot for lunch after you've visited some wineries, picked grapes, or taken a trail ride at Painted Bar Stables. They have indoor seating, but their outside deck offers beautiful views of Seneca Lake. For a little place, they offer quite a large menu. You have many choices of creative paninis, salads, and subs, which are all served with chips and a pickle.

26. BAKERIES

Stumbling upon a tiny bakery, opening the door, and being greeted by the smell of freshly baked bread is undeniably inviting. Small bakeries always seem more enticing to me. With steamed windows from the heat of the ovens, friendly faces behind the counter, and baked goods prepared with care, how could you pass by without stopping?

Skaneateles Bakery, located in the charming village of Skaneateles, completely fits that description. Grab a cup of coffee or hot chocolate at the counter and enjoy one of their housemade pop tarts, donuts, or scones. They also serve classic bakery items, such as whoopie pies, assorted cookies, and cupcakes. All of their items are made daily from scratch.

Traveling south to Binghamton, Bread in the Wild is a small artisan bakery, operated by one baker. His bread is all made with wild yeast (hence the "wild" in the name), otherwise known as sourdough. Needless to say, all of the varieties of sourdough breads are top-notch. Without exaggerating, I can honestly say that he also makes the best cinnamon buns in the whole world! Yes, they are really that good! His cruffins are also an amazing breakfast treat that are laced with buttery, sugary goodness! Bread in the Wild produces a variety of baked goods, including some special seasonal choices. You can visit their booth at the Broome County Farmers Market, purchase their products at Old Barn Market in Binghamton, or visit their website.

A little further north, in the Central Region, La Maison Blanche Bakery Cafe is an authentic French bakery located in Norwich. Their cases are filled with mouth-watering French desserts and baked goods. Some of their specialties include pastries, baguettes, and 14 different types of croissants. While picking up your baked goods, you may want to stay and have one of their crepes for lunch!

27. COOKING CLASSES

Sometimes a fun way to experience regional foods is to learn how to make them, from local chefs. There are businesses, both large and small, that offer cooking classes. Rue Claire, in Lodi, listed by Zagat as one of eight reasons to drive to the Finger Lakes, offers chocolate making classes throughout the year. The chocolatier, who studied the art of chocolate making in Paris and Quebec, will immediately make you feel as if you've known her forever. She creates a welcoming, relaxed atmosphere during her classes.

Rue Claire also offers u-pick lavender and a champagne bar called Bubblery. Here, guests can enjoy drinks made from local, organic fruits and herbs. You can also stay at their glamping bed and breakfast, called Bin 414. The site features a wine barrel inspired cabin, outdoor kitchen, fire pit, and nature spa. Rue Claire's social media pages publicize details on upcoming classes.

Also in the Finger Lakes Region, New York Kitchen, in Canandaigua, offers numerous cooking classes for both adults only and families. Adult classes range from learning how to cook en papillote to pizza and wings workshops. Families might enjoy cookie or pizza decorating classes. They also offer fun wine and beer pairing/tasting events, at their state of the art facility at the tip of Canandaigua Lake.

Cornell Cooperative Extension offers a wide variety of hands-on cooking classes for children and adults. Classes are taught in many locations around the NYS. To find the classes, search online for Cornell Cooperative Extension cooking classes and the location that you will be visiting. Classes can range from Italian cookie baking to themed children's events.

28. FESTIVALS

There are so many festivals in New York State! In my opinion, great festivals include fun music, craftspeople selling quality products, and interesting food options. There is such a wide variety of festivals in NYS. I've listed several below, with a few highlights of each festival.

<u>Colorscape Chenango Arts Festival in Norwich</u> - A huge Arts festival in mid-September, featuring fine art and crafts, acoustic music, and hands-on activities. The Wild Owl Cafe is a tasty place for lunch in Norwich.

<u>Spiedie Fest and Balloon Rally in Binghamton</u> - A large festival in August celebrating everything about spiedies. If you get there in the early morning, you can also see the hot air balloon launches.

<u>Ithaca Festival in Ithaca</u> - An eclectic craft fair held in mid-June. Enjoy any number of food options from the food trucks and street vendors, or wander the Ithaca Commons and choose from a large number of local restaurants.

<u>Strawberry Festival in Owego</u> - This festival, held in late June, celebrates everything about the local Strawberry harvest. Offerings include strawberry shortcake, strawberry soup, and strawberry daiquiris.

The non-alcoholic strawberry coolers topped with whipped cream are a perennial favorite!

Sterling Renaissance Festival in Sterling - Tucked into a wooded area, the Renaissance Festival will take you back in time, as you watch jousts and interact with costumed performers. Food options include huge turkey legs and soups and salads in bread bowls. You can even make reservations to have afternoon tea with Queen Elizabeth I!

Lucille Ball Comedy Festival in Jamestown - This festival features over 50 events and dozens of well-known performers who honor the craft of comedy. Many well-known comedians headline at the comedy festival. While in Jamestown you can grab lunch or dinner at Havana Cuban Cafe and Pizzeria or Labyrinth Press Company.

29. FUN FOODIE DESTINATIONS COMBINED WITH GREAT MUSIC

As a musician by trade, I'm always thrilled when I come across an eatery with *good* live music. Wineries consistently have quality live music on the weekends and at special events. Events at wineries are plentiful in the Summer and Fall, so check the calendars on their websites for live music schedules. Some other suggestions of places where great food and great music mix are listed below.

Lost Dog Cafe and Lounge in Binghamton - Lost Dog customers are an eclectic mix of college students, local families, and business people. In addition to their live music and weekly jazz jams, they also serve fantastic dinners and drinks.

The Chautauqua Institution in Chautauqua - The Chautauqua Institution is a relaxing and inspirational location to visit in the summer. The concerts, recitals, ballets, and operas are all very high quality. They often attract well-known musicians who give performances and lectures. There are five dining establishments at The Chautauqua Institute. They range from the upscale dining at Heirloom Restaurant at The Athenaeum Hotel, to coffee and ice cream at Brick Walk Cafe.

Broadway in NYC - You can see top-notch musical theater in many cities around the United States. However, the thrill of walking into an old Broadway theater to watch a live show will never get old. For the hours that you are in the theater, the outside world ceases to exist, while you are enveloped in glorious song and dance. There are a plethora of restaurants in the theater district that cater to both pre and post-show diners. Sardi's is one of the iconic restaurants in the heart of the theater district. Everyone should go there at least once, to sit among the caricatures of celebrities, and eat classic dishes, such as Shrimp Sardi and Orange Teriyaki Glazed Grilled Salmon.

30. DESSERT

Many of my favorite dessert spots coincide with my favorite places for meals. In NYS, desserts can range anywhere from candy apples to Victorian Sponge. Here are some of the more delectable offerings in NYS:

Tea and Sympathy in the West Village - Yes, Tea and Sympathy is mentioned in several categories of this book. Their food is just that good! Their authentic English desserts include freshly baked Victoria Sponge and Sticky Toffee Pudding.

Patisserie in Skaneateles - Patisserie is located in an old carriage house behind The Sherwood Inn, in downtown Skaneateles. They sell enticing french desserts, along with breakfast goodies, and breads. Their warm Stretch Bread is amazing! After purchasing a dessert, take it across the street to Clift Park and enjoy views of Skaneateles Lake.

One Ring Donuts in Ithaca - Donuts are traditionally a breakfast food, but the goodies at One Ring Donuts are so decadent they can definitely be dessert. They make seasonally inspired donuts, using potatoes in their dough. One Ring Donuts always has at least one vegan and gluten-free option, as well.

Coffeehouses are also favorite places to get desserts. Most have housemade desserts or goodies from local bakeries.

31. ITALIAN RESTAURANTS

Italian food gets its own category because there are so many amazing Italian restaurants across NYS! One of my favorites is Barstow House in Nichols. The family-run restaurant is housed in a renovated 175-year-old home. Their homemade pasta and bread is prepared with care, and is a treat! Insider tip - Barstow House is located near Fainting Goat Island

Inn, which is ranked as one of New York State's most haunted hotels!

Traveling toward the tip of Long Island, is Il Capuccino, in Sag Harbor. The Hamptons are historically not known for being the most inexpensive place to visit. However, Il Capuccino is a cozy, affordable option in downtown Sag Harbor. The servers are kind, the food scrumptious and plentiful, and children are welcomed! This is a restaurant where you may feel more comfortable in business casual attire.

In the Central NY town of Cortland, is Melodyland Restaurant. When you walk in Melodyland, their retro decor makes you feel as if you are in another era. They offer classic, home-cooked Italian foods, with very generous portions.

There are several cities in New York, both large and small, that have Little Italy sections. The most obvious large city choice is the Little Italy neighborhood of Manhattan. Ask a group of native New Yorkers where their favorite restaurant is in Little Italy, and you'll probably get several different answers. The restaurants are plentiful, and street festivals are crowded, but fun. For small cities, Endicott's Oak Hill area boasts a thriving Italian cultural area. Consol's Family Kitchen and Joey's

Pizzeria and Italian Ice have been favorites of locals for decades. If you're on Oak Hill, be sure to go to Battaglini Bakery for freshly baked Italian bread.

32. SAMPLE FOOD FROM ANOTHER COUNTRY

One way that I helped my daughter learn about different countries and cultures was to spend days, or even weeks, where we prepared recipes from a chosen country. Sometimes, we also went to restaurants that specialized in food from different countries. Some of our favorite places are:

Basha's Lebanese Grill in Vestal - Basha's is owned by a family of four, who make everyone feel welcome. Everything on their menu is good! Some of our favorites are tabouli salad, baba ghanoush, chicken tawook, and chicken shawarma.

Royal Indian Bar and Grill in Vestal - Royal Indian has an extensive menu of classic Indian dishes. They even allow you to adjust the spice level for your palette. I am typically not a fan of buffets, but their weekday buffet lunch is great and allows you to sample many different kinds of foods.

Eva's European Sweets in Syracuse - Eva's serves authentic Polish Cuisine in a homey, relaxed setting. The menu includes various types of pierogi, placki, and goulash, along with amazing desserts..

Hai Hong in Ithaca - Hai Hong, in the Collegetown area of Ithaca, serves traditional Chinese meals and dim sum. If you've never ordered dim sum, the servers are all happy to explain the menu. If you want to make your visit extra special, ask if Thomas is there!

Las Chicas Taqueria in Owego - Las Chicas serves West Coast Style Tacos, Smothered Burritos, Burrito Bowls, and Nachos. Their deck overlooking Owego's Riverwalk and the Susquehanna River is a beautiful and relaxing spot for lunch or dinner.

Hawi Ethiopian Cuisine in Ithaca - Hawi is located just off the Commons area of Ithaca. They serve Ethiopian foods in the traditional way. Every entree comes with spongy teff flatbread, which you use to scoop up your food. Utensils are available upon request. Hawi encourages diners to order a few different items and share them family-style. Their menu features many vegetarian dishes, along with meat entrees.

NYC has a plethora of restaurants highlighting different cultures. Try a Korean BBQ, gelato in Little Italy, or traditional Jewish comfort food at Russ and Daughters Cafe.

33. EATING OUT, WITH FOOD ALLERGIES

Many members of my family, including myself, have food allergies ranging from soy to shellfish to chocolate. Over the years, we have found that some restaurants are much better about accommodating food allergies than others. I've spent hours researching which restaurants are allergy-friendly, prior to going on trips to other states or overseas. In general, if you call ahead and are honest about what your needs are, I've found that most family-owned businesses are happy to accommodate. A few restaurants that are reliably allergy friendly are:

Old Mill Restaurant in Mt. Upton - Old Mill, housed in a former grist mill on Unadilla River, has been in business for over 70 years. They serve lunch and dinner and offer gluten-free meals.

Carol's Coffee and Art Bar in Owego - You can read the Coffeehouse section for more information on Carol's, but they offer many gluten-friendly menu items. They even have homemade gluten-free desserts and breakfast items.

Whole in the Wall in Binghamton - This little restaurant has been a fixture in the Southern Tier for decades. They advertise themselves as a "natural" restaurant and serve a variety of international foods. They have vegan/vegetarian dishes and are very happy to accommodate special dietary needs. Their pesto is legendary and is sold at the restaurant, Broome County Farmers Market, and many grocery stores.

Waffle Frolic in Ithaca - Waffle Frolic, located on the Ithaca Commons, often has a line out the door on the weekends! They serve yummy sweet and savory waffles, and more. Waffle Frolic takes food allergies very seriously and also offers gluten-free and vegan options.

34. FISH AND CHIPS ON THIS SIDE OF THE POND

We greatly enjoyed sampling fish and chips on our trips to England and Ireland. While nothing beats the smell of frying fish in a chippy in the UK, there are a few places in NYS that will rival the fish and chips from across the pond! A Salt & Battery, in the West Village, serves traditional British fish and chips, with a side of mushy peas if you would like. The restaurant only has a few seats, so I recommend getting your order to go and taking it to one of the many parks in the Village. In Central NY and the Finger Lakes Regions, you'll find Doug's Fish Fry in Skaneateles and Cortland have a devoted following. People flock to their brick and mortar locations, with lines typically stretching down the sidewalk. They also have a roaming food truck that pops up at various locations. Also in the Finger Lakes Region, is Northstar House, in Ithaca. I could have included Northstar under the best brunch or pub, as well. It's a quirky, relaxed restaurant with loads of outdoor seating, and fish and chips is just one of the amazing foods they make!

35. NYS COOKBOOKS

When I'm traveling, I often try to pick up a cookbook from the area. Sometimes I find regional cookbooks, but often, individual restaurants are so good that I want to attempt their recipes at home. One of my favorite restaurants, Moosewood, (see their information under Vegetarian/Vegan Restaurants) also produces some of my favorite cookbooks. As of 2020, they have released 14 cookbooks sharing many of their amazing vegetarian dishes.

Tea and Sympathy produces another of my favorite cookbooks. The book, written by one of the first waitresses at Tea and Sympathy, is part biography of the eatery and part cookbook. All of the recipes were shared by the owner, and most are currently served at Tea and Sympathy.

Farmers Markets are also great places to pick up cookbooks. I have several cookbooks produced by farmers markets, with an overview of recipes that you can make with locally sourced meat and produce. Some farmers markets offer cookbooks at a very low cost, or free of charge, at their information booths. Often, u-pick farms and produce stands will also offer free recipe booklets featuring their fruits and vegetables.

36. AMISH FARMS AND SHOPS

People generally think of Pennsylvania when they hear of Amish communities in the United States. However, in certain regions, NYS has quite a large population of Amish families. Amish farms often have roadside stands, selling maple syrup, honey, produce, and baked goods. Some of the larger stands even sell hand-sewn products and handmade furniture. The Pulaski area, Newark Valley and Candor areas, Finger Lakes region, and Cattaraugus County all have many Amish Farms. Cattaraugus County even has a website dedicated to an Amish trail of shops.

There are a few courtesies to remember when you are around Amish farms. They do not sell anything on Sundays and do not accept credit cards. Sometimes there won't even be a person working at the stand, but instead, there will be a price list and a box in which to deposit money. While we might think it's exciting to see Amish families working on their farms, please do not invade their privacy and take photographs. Just enjoy their homemade products, and if given the chance, chat for a bit.

37. ICE CREAM

Sure, Vermont has Ben and Jerry's, but New York has an abundance of family-owned ice cream shops, producing their own ice cream. Here are a few of my favorites:

Ice Cream Works in Owego - Ice Cream Works is housed in the old Kies Bottling Works factory, in The Flats area of Owego. Ice Cream Works serves several homemade flavors, along with Perry's hard ice cream, Dole whip, slushies, and Icebergs (slushies topped with soft serve vanilla). Homemade flavors change frequently, but some favorites include:

Sweater Weather - Apple ice cream base, chunks of cinnamon donut, and caramel

Christmas Cookie - Vanilla ice cream base, red and green sprinkles, pieces of sugar cookie, and swirls of buttercream frosting

Blueberry Crumble - Blueberry ice cream base (made with freshly picked local blueberries) and homemade crumble topping.

Ice Cream Works also offers beautifully decorated ice cream cakes, ice cream sandwiches, and ice cream flights.

Purity Ice Cream in Ithaca - Purity has been making ice cream in Ithaca since 1936. If you aren't able to make it to their Ithaca store, you can purchase their ice cream and eggnog in many grocery stores. Some of the fun flavors at Purity include:

Almond Joyous -- Coconut ice cream, fudge, and roasted chopped almonds

Cookie Dough After Dark – Chocolate ice cream, cookie dough, chocolate chunks, and caramel s

Peppermint - Mint flavored ice cream with red & green peppermint candies

Purity also carries yummy ice cream cakes and baked goods.

Cayuga Lake Creamery in Interlaken - Cayuga Lake Creamery produces small-batch ice cream, made on-site with local ingredients They have an extensive menu, which changes frequently. Some of their unique choices include:

Banore - Banana and Oreo

Maple Bacon - Made with local maple syrup and caramelized bacon

S'mores - Filled with graham crackers, chocolate chunks, mini marshmallows, marshmallow swirls, and fudge

<u>Taylor Marie's Ice Cream Parlor in Pulaski</u> - Taylor Marie's serves not only homemade ice cream but homemade waffle cones and dishes, as well. The sweet aroma of the freshly made waffle cones greets you as soon as you arrive! You can choose from plain, chocolate dipped, or chocolate-dipped with sprinkles. Some of the local favorites at Taylor Marie's are American Cookies and Cream (with red, white, and blue Oreos), Strawberry Cheesecake, and Pistachio.

38. SEASONAL SUGGESTIONS

Every season in NYS brings its own joys. Summer is the busiest tourist season in most locations, but with all of the options in NYS, you may want to time your visit for Spring, Fall, or Winter. The next few categories offer suggestions for foodie options according to each season.

Spring

CNY Maple Festival in Marathon - As the name implies this festival, held in early April, offers tastes of everything maple. You can take home maple cotton candy, maple candy, and maple syrup.

Ramps are wild leeks that are foraged in Upstate NY. They are quite popular and sell out very quickly at Farmers markets. In the Spring, they are a common ingredient in dishes at Farm to Table restaurants. Ramps add a delicious flavor and texture to any number of dishes. I love ramps in ravioli and stir fry.

Flower shows - Many gardens and horticultural centers offer Spring shows. Check out New York Botanical Garden (two great eateries on the grounds), Brooklyn Botanic Garden (Japanese food specialties), Macy's Flower Show (cafes in and around Macy's), Rochester Lilac Show (wine tasting and brewfest), or the Capital District Garden and Flower Show (NYS wine tastings and cafe food).

39. SUMMER

Summer affords numerous opportunities no matter where you are. Look at regional websites for a festival, outdoor concert, or seasonal food truck. One of my favorite things to do in the summer is to order a picnic lunch from a local cafe and head to a lake or waterfall. A few of my favorite picnic locations and cafes are:

Cazenovia Lake - Pewter Spoon Cafe in Cazenovia

Taughannock Falls by Cayuga Lake in Trumansburg - Collegetown Bagels at three locations in Ithaca

Watkins Glen State Park, or Clute Park on Seneca Lake in Watkins Glen - Glen Mountain Market Bakery and Deli for lunch, and Seneca Sunrise Coffee for the best iced coffee in Watkins Glen

40. AUTUMN

Autumn in New York is known for cider donuts, candy apples, and pumpkin farms. Historically there have been apple orchards from Long Island across the state to Lake Ontario, and down to the Pennsylvania border. Naturally, u-pick apples, as well as grape and pumpkin picking are favorite Fall activities in NYS.

67

Some fun suggestions for other Autumn activities in NYS are:

Stoughton Farm Corn Maze in Newark Valley - The maze is cut into an elaborate picture, which is different every year. This is a fun, family activity that you can do any time of day. Completing the maze after dark adds an added sense of fun for older children! You can also purchase hot cider, freshly made donuts, and a variety of baked goods and produce.

The Cider Mill in Endicott - The Cider Mill has been a fixture in the Southern Tier for generations. When you enter the mill, you can take a short, self-guided tour to watch donuts being made, and apples being squeezed in the presses to make cider. In addition to numerous kinds of donuts and cider, they also sell candy apples and homemade pies.

LaFayette (early October) and Ithaca (late September) Apple Festivals - The festivals are both large events celebrating the apple harvest. They are filled with craft booths and a wide variety of apple foods and ciders.

41. WINTER

Yes, Winter in NYS means cold and snow. Depending on where you are, snowfalls range anywhere from a few inches to a few feet. However, there are still loads of fun things to do in the Winter, in NYS!

A couple of perennially favorite activities are:

Dickens Christmas in Skaneateles - This yearly tradition begins the weekend after Thanksgiving and continues every weekend until Christmas. The weekends see this quaint lakeside village transformed into a Victorian town, with costumed actors and horse-drawn wagon rides. You can hear Charles Dickens tell the tale of *A Christmas Carol,* carol by the lake with Queen Victoria (be sure to stay until the end to sing a rousing rendition of The 12 Days of Christmas), or get your picture taken with Father Christmas. While you're strolling the village, you will be offered samples of eggnog and roasted chestnuts. For lunch, you can head inside Gilda's for artisan pizza and salad. If you would like to warm up with a drink and a treat, grab a cup of Vermont Green Mountain Coffee and some delectable chocolates at Vermont Green Mountain Specialty Co.

Corning Glass Museum in Corning - Corning Glass Museum offers glass blowing classes many different times of the year, but during the holidays, you can make your own glass-blown Christmas ornament. The classes are appropriate for any age, last less than an hour, and typically cost around $30. After making your own ornament and exploring the museum, head over to Soul Full Cup Coffeehouse, on Market Street, for a latte or quick bite. If you're looking for lunch or dinner, try Old World Cafe, Hand and Foot, or Market Street Brewing Company.

42. NYS BY REGION

You may want to explore NYS by region. Here are some other great foodie spots in many of the popular tourist regions of NYS. You can also refer to the individual sections in this book for other recommendations.

Adirondacks - The Adirondacks are located in the North-Eastern part of NYS, and are a place where many people escape the hustle and bustle of everyday life. Lake George, Whiteface Mountain, Old Forge, and Saranac Lake are popular tourist spots. Some tried and true local favorite Adirondack restaurants are:

Tony Harper's Pizza and Clam Shack - Lowville and Old Forge

The Oxbow Inn - Piseco

Screamen Eagle - Inlet

Noon Mark Diner - Keene Valley

Nina's Sweet Shoppe - Lake George

Wheatfield's Restaurant and Bar - Saratoga Springs and Clifton Park

43. CAPITAL – SARATOGA REGION

This region includes New York State's capital, Albany, as well as Saratoga Springs. This area is home to the Saratoga Performing Arts Center, Saratoga Race Course, and the historic Saratoga Spa State Park. In Albany, you can visit The New York State Museum, with permanent exhibits on 9/11 and the wildlife of NYS. Be sure to take a ride on the carousel on the 4th floor!

Some favorite restaurants are:

Grapevine Farms - Cobleskill

Katie O'Byrne's Irish Pub - Schenectady

Hattie's Restaurant - Saratoga Springs

Wheatfields Restaurant and Bar - Saratoga Springs and Clifton Park

Albany Pump Station - Albany

The Olde English Pub and Pantry - Albany

44. CATSKILL REGION

The Catskills in the South-Eastern part of New York State have long been a favorite escape for people living in NYC. This region is home to the Catskill Preserve, with mountains, lakes, and miles of trails. Some favorite places to eat in this area include:

Roscoe Diner - right next to Route 17 in Roscoe (This diner has been a fixture for decades, and a favorite stop for those traveling between Upstate and NYC.)

Quickway Diner - Bloomingburg

Kaatskeller Restaurant - Livingston Manor

The Old Schoolhouse Inn and Restaurant - Downsville

R&R Taproom - Woodstock

Peekamoose Restaurant - Big Indian

45. CENTRAL NEW YORK REGION

Directly in the center of NYS, this area is known for The National Baseball Hall of Fame, Erie Canal Boat Cruises, and Howes Caverns. There are also many lakes, state parks, and theaters in the area. This region also contains what is known as the Southern Tier, which is an area that borders Pennsylvania. A few favorite restaurants in this region include:

Funk 'n Waffles - Syracuse (Featured on the show *Diners, Drive-Ins, and Dives*, they serve savory and sweet waffles with vegetarian options)

Pastabilities - Syracuse

Remlik's - Binghamton

The Colonial - Binghamton

Quack's Village Inn - Madison

Main Street Grill and Bakery - Afton

Frank's Italian Restaurant - Maine

Strong Hearts - Syracuse

46. CHAUTAUQUA – ALLEGHENY REGION AND GREAT NIAGARA REGION

These areas encompass the Westernmost part of New York State, bordering Pennsylvania to the south and Canada to the north. The regions include Allegheny and Lake Erie State Parks, and Niagara Falls. Some of the well-known eateries in this area include:

Heirloom Restaurant in the Athenaeum Hotel at Chautauqua Institute - Chautauqua

The Horseshoe Inn - Frewsburg

The Hide-A-Way - Steamburg

The Old Library Restaurant and Inn - Olean

Buffalo Wing Trail - 12 locations in and around Buffalo, including the famous Anchor Bar in Buffalo

Schwabl's - Buffalo

47. FINGER LAKES REGION

This region stretches from the shores of Lake Ontario, through all of the Finger Lakes, and down to the Pennsylvania border. Entire books have been written about this area, and many suggestions are sprinkled throughout this book, as well. A few other options that have not been mentioned in other sections are:

Wine, Cheese, Brewery, Distillery, and Cider trails - check NY travel websites for free trail maps and special events

Mia - Ithaca

Tamarind - Ithaca

Rio Tomatlan - Canandaigua

Village Tavern Restaurant and Inn - Hammondsport

New York Pizzeria & Restaurant - New Berlin

Mom's Savona Diner - Savona

Fargo Bar and Grill - Aurora

Pietro & Son Italian Restaurant - Elmira

48. HUDSON VALLEY

The Hudson Valley area is in the Southeastern part of the state and is the region closest to NYC. This area is known for its top-rate gardens, well-known music festivals, and the world's longest pedestrian bridge. A few options for dining in this area are:

Culinary Institute of America - Hyde Park - restaurants at the Culinary Institute of America include American Bounty Restaurant, The Bocuse

Restaurant, Ristorante Caterina de' Medici, Apple Pie
Bakery Cafe

Cosimo's Brick Oven - Newburgh

Pegasus Restaurant - Coxsackie

Main Street Bistro - New Paltz

Verdigris Tea and Chocolate - Hudson

49. NYC AND LONG ISLAND

This is another area that countless books have been
written about. NYC and Long Island are filled with
museums, performances, shopping, and historical
sites. I have included many NYC suggestions
throughout this book, and you may also want to
consult Eat Like a Local - New York City. Here are a
few additional suggestions for Long Island, which are
not included in other sections of this book:

Maroni's - Northport

Maureen's Kitchen - Smithtown

Munday's - Huntington

Broadway Dinette - Huntington

Flour and Oak - Staten Island

Tiger Lily Cafe - Port Jefferson

50. THOUSAND ISLAND – SEAWAY

The Thousand Islands region stretches from the Canadian border all along the Saint Lawrence Seaway. As you might expect, many of the popular activities have something to do with being on, or near, the water. There are many boat cruises, battlefield sites, and state parks in this area. A few suggestions for eating are:

River Rat Cheese - Clayton

Wellesley Hotel Restaurant - Thousand Island Park

The Spot Bistro and Patio - Alexandria Bay

Bella's - Clayton

Clipper Inn - Clayton

BONUS TIPS

BONUS TIP #1

I have included a few NYS recipes for you to try at home. You may want to gather ingredients for them on your trip to NYS!

Spiedie Marinade
2 cups olive oil

1 cup white vinegar

2 Tbsp. lemon juice

5 cloves minced garlic

2 tsp. dried oregano

1 Tbsp. garlic salt

3 Tbsp crushed mint

2 Tbsp. basil

1 tsp. black pepper

Combine all ingredients in a large bowl. Add about 5 lbs of your choice of meat, and marinate overnight. Spiedies taste the best cooked on a grill!

Empire State Muffins

2 cups shredded unpeeled apples

1 ⅓ cup sugar

1 cup chopped cranberries

1 cup shredded carrots

1 cup chopped walnuts

2 ½ cups flour

1 Tbsp. baking powder

2 tsp. baking soda

2 tsp. Cinnamon

2 eggs, lightly beaten

½ cup vegetable oil or applesauce

In a large mixing bowl, combine apples and sugar. Gently fold in cranberries, carrots, and nuts. Combine dry ingredients; add to the mixing bowl. Mix well to moisten dry ingredients. Combine eggs and oil/applesauce and stir into apple mixture.

Pour into greased muffin tins and bake at 375 degrees for 20-25 minutes.

Apple Crunch

Butter a 13x9 inch pan. Peel and slice 8 medium apples into the pan. Make a syrup of 1 cup maple syrup and 1/2 cup water. Pour over the apples.

Mix together 1 tsp. Cinnamon, 1 cup flour, ½ cup butter, and ½ cup brown sugar. Sprinkle mixture over the apples. Bake at 350 degrees, for 1 hour. Eat plain, or with a scoop of locally made vanilla ice cream.

Pesto

2 cups of packed basil, or any combination of basil, ramps, and chives
4 cloves of garlic
¼ -⅓ cup of olive oil
½ cup of Parmesan Cheese
Salt and pepper to taste

Add all ingredients, except the olive oil, to a food processor or blender. Add olive oil a little at a time, and continue to blend until you have the desired consistency. You can freeze this pesto and take it out as needed, for topping pasta, meats, or vegetables.

BONUS TIP #2

There are some locations that you might not think of as food destinations, but they offer a fun activity and tasty treats. A few of my favorites include:

<u>Cinemapolis in Ithaca</u> - Yes, a movie theatre for food! Their popcorn is air-popped and each helping is seasoned to order. Gourmet toppings include, but are not limited to local flavored Olive Oil from F. Oliver's store, old Bay Seasoning, Nutritional Yeast, and of course the traditional natural butter and salt. They also have brewed coffee, iced tea, and ice creams.

<u>Carousels in the Southern Tier</u> - Carousels have been a free summertime activity for generations of families from the Southern Tier. You can find a map to all of the carousel parks online. After your ride each of the carousels, ask the attendant for a carousel card. You can turn the cards in after your last carousel ride and get a pin commemorating your carousel tour. After spending a day riding carousels, head to one of the many Italian restaurants on the Northside of Endicott. Insider tip - Some of the carousels have a pig and dog mixed in with the horses. These are the sought after animals on those particular carousels. Children always race to claim a ride on the pink pig or brown dog!

<u>Path Through History</u> - New York State's Path Through History can be found online, or on pamphlets in many tourism offices. Through this "path," you can explore New York's rich heritage. For instance, you might want to learn more about Women's Rights by visiting Seneca Falls, which is known as the birthplace of the Women's Rights Movement in the United States. Other locations include the Harriet Tubman National Historic Park in Auburn, Revolutionary War sites, and the various Theodore, Franklin, and Eleanor Roosevelt sites. Of course, you should explore all that local eateries have to offer no matter what historical site you choose to visit!

BONUS TIP #3

NYC is one of the best cities in the United States to experience fine music. You are just as likely to hear top-notch music in Central Park, or the subway, as you are in a concert hall. One of the best jazz saxophonists I've heard was performing on the Mall in Central Park. You may want to purchase tickets to a Broadway musical, NY Philharmonic Concert, or Metropolitan Opera. However, I also encourage you to take time as you are walking through Central Park or Washington Square Park to stop and listen to the variety of performers. Some will be selling cd's or just asking for donations. If you have enjoyed a group, I would encourage you to support them, by throwing a dollar (or five) into their tip jar. After you've strolled through Central Park, grab a drink and a quick snack at The Todd English Food Hall at The Plaza Hotel!

Whatever you decide to do, and wherever you decide to go in New York State, be sure to take time to wonder over small surprises and enjoy the sheer gift of travel!

READ OTHER BOOKS BY CZYK PUBLISHING

Greater Than a Tourist- St. Croix US Birgin Islands USA: 50 Travel Tips from a Local by Tracy Birdsall

Greater Than a Tourist- Toulouse France: 50 Travel Tips from a Local by Alix Barnaud

Children's Book: *Charlie the Cavalier Travels the World* by Lisa Rusczyk

Eat Like a Local

Follow *Eat Like a Local on* Amazon.

Join our mailing list for new books

http://bit.ly/EatLikeaLocalbooks

Printed in Great Britain
by Amazon

14821374R00058